OBJECT ORIENTED PROGRAMMING

OBJECT ORIENTED PROGRAMMING - I

DR. MANMOHAN SINGH | RAHUL SHARMA | ANKIT CHAKRAWARTI

This book is dedicated to help educators teach classes in the OOP. It introduces OOP and their application or uses in learning.

Contents

Foreword

It is a pleasure to write this foreword to the book Object-Oriented Programming, co-authored by two of my former colleagues, Rahul Sharma and Ankit Chakrawarti. Both of them have several years, of experience in teaching various subjects related to computer technology. They have clearly brought their teaching expertise into effect in writing this book which emphasizes the learning of fundamental concepts as well as the application of these concepts to develop efficient object-oriented programs for solving problems in various fields.

Preface

Welcome to the world of object-oriented programming using C++ and Java. Get ready for an exciting tour!

While teaching OOPs, C++ and Java to graduate and postgraduate students and practicing professionals from the industry for several years, our experience shows that:

There are good programmers both in C++ and Java but very few among them understand the underlying OOPs concepts.

The text books available treat C++, Java and OOPs concepts as different and separate and students get exposed to these concepts in a compartmentalized manner.

The study of OOPs languages, analysis and design and software development are all treated separately thereby sacrificing the integrated OOPs approach.

C++ is a highly evolved language and is used in systems

Acknowledgements

We would like to express our gratitude to all the professors and researchers who contributed to this, our first, book and to all those who provided support, talked things over, or read, wrote, and offered comments.

Unit I

Introduction to Object Oriented Programming: Object oriented paradigm-Differences between Object Oriented Programming and Procedure oriented programming, Basic concepts of Object Oriented Programming, Encapsulation, Inheritance and Polymorphism, Benefits of OOP, Structure of a C++ program, namespace, Data types, C++ tokens, Identifiers, Variables, Constants, Operators, Control structures & Loops.

Unit-II

Functions, Classes and Objects: Introduction of Classes, Class Definition, Defining a Members,Objects,Access Control, Class Scope, Scope Resolution Operator, Inline functions, Memory Allocation for Objects, Static Data Members, Static Member Functions, Arrays of Objects, Objects as Function Arguments, Friend Functions.

Unit-III

Constructors, Destructors, Inheritance: Introduction to Constructors, Default Constructors, Parameterized Constructors, Copy Constructors, Multiple Constructors in a Class, Destructors.

Inheritance: Introduction to inheritance, Defining Derived Classes, Single Inheritance, Multiple Inheritance, Multi level Inheritance, Hierarchical Inheritance, Hybrid Inheritance.

Unit-IV

Pointers, Virtual Functions and Polymorphism:

Introduction to Memory management, new operator and delete operator, Pointers to objects, Pointers to Derived Classes, Polymorphism, Compile time polymorphism, Run time polymorphism, Virtual Functions, Overloading-Function Overloading, Operator overloading.

Unit-V

Templates and Exception handling: Introduction to Templates, Class Templates, Class Templates with Multiple Parameters, Function Templates, Function Templates with Multiple Parameters. **Exception handling:** Basics of Exception Handling, Types of exceptions, Exception Handing Mechanism, Throwing and Catching Mechanism, Rethrowing an Exception, Specifying Exceptions.

CHAPTER ONE

Concepts of Object Oriented programming

Overview of C language:

1.C language is known as structure oriented language or procedure oriented language

2. Employs top-down programming approach where a problem is viewed as a sequence of tasks to be performed.

3. All program code of c can be executed in C++ but converse many not be possible

4. Function overloading and operator overloading are not possible.

5. Local variables can be declared only at the beginning of the block.

6. Program controls are through jumps and calls to subroutines. 7.Polymorphism, encapsulation and inheritance are not possible.

For solving the problems, the problem is divided into a number of modules. Each module is a subprogram.

8. Data abstraction property is not supported by procedure oriented language.

9. Data in procedure oriented language is open and can be accessed by any function.

Overview of C++ language:

1. C++ can be considered as an incremental version of c language which consists all programming language constructs with newly added features of object oriented programming.

2. c++ is structure(procedure) oriented and object oriented programming language. 3.The file extension of C++ program is ".CPP"

4. Function overloading and operator overloading are possible.

5. Variables can be declared in inline i.e when required

6. In c++ more emphasis is give on data rather than procedures

7. Polymorphism, encapsulation and inheritance are possible.

8. Data abstraction property is supported by c++.

9. Data access is limited. It can be accessed by providing various visibility modes both for data and member functions. there by providing data security by data hiding

10. Dymanic binding is supported by C++ 11..It supports all features of c language

12. It can be called as an incremental version of c language

Difference Between Procedure Oriented Programming (POP) & Object Oriented Programming (OOP)

Procedure Oriented Programming:

1. Program is divided into small parts called functions. 2. Importance is not given to data but to functions as well as sequence of actions to be done. 3. Follows Top Down approach. 4. It does not have any access specifier. 5. Data can move freely from function to function in the system. 6. Most function uses Global data for sharing that can be accessed freely from function to function in the system.

7. Overloading is not possible. 8. Example of Procedure Oriented Programming are : C, VB, FORTRAN, Pascal.

Object Oriented Programming:

1. Program is divided into parts called objects. 2. Importance is given to the data rather than procedures or functions because it works as a real world. 3. OOP follows Bottom Up approach. 4. OOP has access specifiers named Public, Private, Protected, etc. 5. Objects can move and communicate with each other through member functions. 6. In OOP, data can not move easily from function to function,it can be kept public or private so we can control the access of data. 7. In OOP, overloading is possible in the form of Function Overloading and Operator Overloading. 8. Example of Object Oriented Programming are : C++, JAVA, VB.NET, C#.NET.

Principles(or features) of object oriented programming:

1. Encapsulation
2. Data abstraction
3. Polymorphism
4. Inheritance
5. Dynamic binding
6. Message passing

Encapsulation: Wrapping of data and functions together as a single unit is known as encapsulation. By default data is not accessible to outside world and they are only accessible through the functions which are wrapped in a class. prevention of data direct access by the program is called data hiding or information hiding

Data abstraction : Abstraction refers to the act of representing essential features without including the back ground details or explanation. Classes use the concept of abstraction and are defined as a list of attributes such as size, weight, cost and functions to operate on these attributes. They encapsulate all essential properties of the object that are to be created. The attributes are called as data members as they hold data and the functions which operate on these data are called as member functions.

Class use the concept of data abstraction so they are called abstract data type (ADT)

Polymorphism: Polymorphism comes from the Greek words “poly” and “morphism”. “poly” means many and “morphism” means form i.e.. many forms. Polymorphism means the ability to take more than one form. For example, an operation have different behavior in different instances. The behavior depends upon the type of the data used in the operation.

Different ways to achieving polymorphism in C++ program:

1) Function overloading 2) Operator overloading

```
#include<iostream>
using namespace std; int main()
{ int a=4; a=a<<2;
cout<<"a="<<a<<endl; return 0;
}
```

Inheritance: Inheritance is the process by which one object can acquire the properties of another. Inheritance is the most promising concept of OOP, which helps realize the goal of constructing software from reusable parts, rather than hand coding every system from scratch. Inheritance not only supports reuse across systems, but also directly facilitates extensibility within a system. Inheritance coupled with polymorphism and dynamic binding minimizes the amount of existing code to be modified while enhancing a system.

When the class child, inherits the class parent, the class child is referred to as derived class (sub class) and the class parent as a base class (super class). In this case, the class child has two parts: a derived part and an incremental part. The derived part is inherited from the class parent. The incremental part is the new code written specifically for the class child. Dynamic binding: Binding refers to linking of procedure call to the code to be executed in response to the call. Dynamic binding(or late binding) means the code associated with a given procedure call in not known until the time of call at run time.

Message passing: An object oriented program consists of set of object that communicate with each other.

Objects communicates with each other by sending and receiving information .

A message for an object is a request for execution of a procedure and there fore invoke the function that is called for an object and generates result.

Benefits of object oriented programming (OOPs) Reusability: In OOP" s programs functions and modules that are written by a user can be reused by other users without any modification.

Inheritance: Through this we can eliminate redundant code and extend the use of existing classes.

Data Hiding: The programmer can hide the data and functions in a class from other classes. It helps the programmer to build the secure programs.

Reduced complexity of a problem: The given problem can be viewed as a collection of different objects. Each object is responsible for a specific task. The problem is solved by interfacing the objects. This technique reduces the complexity of the program design.

Easy to Maintain and Upgrade: OOP makes it easy to maintain and modify existing code as new objects can be created with small differences to existing ones. Software complexity can be easily managed.

Message Passing: The technique of message communication between objects makes the interface with external systems easier.

Modifiability: it is easy to make minor changes in the data representation or the procedures in an OO program. Changes inside a class do not affect any other part of a program, since the only

public interface that the external world has to a class is through the use of methods.

BASIC STRUCTURE OF C++ LANGUAGE : The program written in C++ language follows this basic structure. The sequence of sections should be as they are in the basic structure. A C program should have one or more sections but the sequence of sections is to be followed. 1. Documentation section

2. Linking section

3. Definition section

4. Global declaration section & class declarations 5.Member function definition

6. Main function

section main()

{

Declaration section Executable section

}

1. DOCUMENTATION SECTION : comes first and is used to document the use of logic or reasons in your program. It can be used to write the program's objective, developer and logic details. The documentation is done in C language with /* and */ . Whatever is written between these two are called comments.

2. LINKING SECTION : This section tells the compiler to link the certain occurrences of keywords or functions in your program to the header files specified in this section.
e.g. #include<iostream>
using namespace std;
-> directive causes the preprocessor to add the contents of the iostream file to the program. It contains declarations for cout and cin.
-> cout is a predefined object that represents the standard output stream. The operator << is an
insertion operator, causes the string in double quotes to be displayed on the screen.

3. DEFINITION SECTION : It is used to declare some constants and assign them some value. e.g. #define MAX 25 Here #define is a compiler directive which tells the compiler whenever MAX is found in the program replace it with 25.

4. GLOBAL DECLARATION SECTION : Here the variables and class definations which are used through out the program (including main and other functions) are declared so as to make them global(i.e accessible to all parts of program). A CLASS is a collection of data and functions that act or manipulate the data. The data components of a class are called data members and function components of a class are called member functions. A class ca also termed as a blue print or prototype that defines the variable or functions common to all objects of certain kind. It is a user defined data type
e.g.
int i; //this declaration is done outside and before main()

5. SUB PROGRAM OR FUNCTION SECTION : This has all the sub programs or the functions which our program needs. void display()

```
{
cout<<"C++ is better that C";
}
```

SIMPLE „C++ " PROGRAM:

```
#include<iostream> using namespace std; void display()
{
cout<<"C++ is better that C";
}
int main()
{
display() return 0;
}
```

6. MAIN FUNCTION SECTION : It tells the compiler where to start the execution from main()

```
{
point from execution starts
}
```

main function has two sections

1. declaration section : In this the variables and their data types are declared.
2. Executable section or instruction section : This has the part of program which actually performs the task we need.

namespace:

namespace is used to define a scope that could hold global identifiers. ex:-namespace scope for c++ standard library.

A classes ,functions and templates are declared within the namespace named std using namespace std;-->directive can be used.

user defined name space:

syntax for defining name space is

```
namespace namespace_name
{
//declarations of variables.functions,classes etc...
```

```
}
ex: #include<iostream> using namespace std; namespace sample
{`
int m;
void display(int n){
cout<<"in namespace N="<<n<<endl;
}
} using namespace sample; int main()
{
int a=5; m=100;
display(200);
cout<<"M in sample name space:"<<sample::m; return 0;}
```

#include<iostream>

This directive causes the preprocessor to add content of iostream file to the program. some old versions of C++ used iostream.h .if complier does not support ANSI (american nation standard institute) C++ then use header file iostream.h

DATA TYPES:

A data type is used to indicate the type of data value stored in a variable. All C compilers support a variety of data types. This variety of data types allows the programmer to select the type appropriate to the needs of the application as well as the machine. ANSI C supports the following classes of data types: 1.Primary (fundamental) data types.
2. Derived data types.
3. User-defined data types

Primary data types:

1. integer data type 2.character data type 3.float point data type 4.Boolean data type 5.void data type

C++ Tokens IDENTIFIERS: Identifiers are the names given to various program elements such as variables, functions and arrays. These are user defined names consisting of sequence of letters and digits.

Rules for declaring identifiers:

The first character must be an alphabet or underscore.

It must consist of only letters, digits and underscore.

Identifiers may have any length but only first 31 characters are significant.

It must not contain white space or blank space.

We should not use keywords as identifiers.

Upper and lower case letters are different.

Example: ab Ab aB AB are treated differently

Examples of valid identifiers:

a, x, n, num, SUM, fact, grand_total, sum_of_digits, sum1

Examples of Invalid identifiers: $amount, ³num′, grand-total, sum of digits, 4num.

$amount : Special character is not permitted grand-total : hyphen is not permitted.

sum of digits : blank spaces between the words are not allowed.

4num : should not start with a number (first character must be a letter or underscore

Note: Some compilers of C recognize only the first 8 characters only; because of this they are unable to distinguish identifiers with the words of length more than eight characters.

Variables:A named memory location is called variable.

OR

It is an identifier used to store the value of particular data type in the memory.

Since variable name is identifier we use following rules which are same as of identifier

Rules for declaring Variables names:

The first character must be an alphabet or underscore.

It must consist of only letters, digits and underscore.
Identifiers may have any length but only first 31 characters are significant.
It must not contain white space or blank space.
We should not use keywords as identifiers.
Upper and lower case letters are different.
Variable names must be unique in the given scope
Ex:int a,b,a;//is in valid
Int a,b;//is valid

Variable declaration: The declaration of variable gives the name for memory location and its size and specifies the range of value that can be stored in that location.
Syntax:
Data type variable name; Ex: int a=10; float x=2.3;

KEYWORDS : There are certain words, called keywords (reserved words) that have a predefined meaning in „C++" language. These keywords are only to be used for their intended purpose and not as identifiers.
The following table shows the standard „C++" keywords.
auto break case char const continue default do double else
enum extern float for goto if int long register return
short signed sizeof static struct switch typedef union unsigned void
volatile while class friend new delete this public private protected inline try throw catch template.

CONSTANTS:
Constants refer to values that do not change during the execution of a program.
Constants can be divided into two major categories:
1. Primary constants:
a) Numeric constants
Integer constants.

Floating-point (real) constants. b)Character constants
Single character constants
String constants
2. Secondary constants:
Enumeration constants.
Symbolic constants.
Arrays, unions, etc.

Rules for declaring constants:

1.Commas and blank spaces are not permitted within the constant. 2.The constant can be preceded by minus (-) signed if required.

3.The value of a constant must be within its minimum bounds of its specified data type.

Integer constants: An integer constant is an integer-valued number. It consists of sequence of digits. Integer constants can be written in three different number systems: 1.Decimal integer (base 10). 2.Octal integer (base 8).
3. Hexadecimal (base 16).

Decimal integer constant: It consists of set of digits, 0 to 9.

Valid declaration: 0, 124, -56, + 67, 4567 etc.

Invalid declaration: $245, 2.34, 34 345, 075. 23,345,00. it is also an invalid declaration.

Note: Embedded spaces, commas, characters, special symbols are not allowed between digits

They can be preceded by an optional + or ± sign.

Octal integer: It consists of set of digits, 0 to 7. Ex: 037, 0, 0765, 05557 etc. (valid representation) It is a sequence of digits preceded by 0.

Ex: Invalid representations

0394: digit 9 is not permitted (digits 0 to 7 only)

235: does not begin with 0. (Leading number must be 0).

Hexadecimal integer: It consists of set of digits, 0 to 9 and alphabets and F. Hexadecimal integer is a sequence of digits preceded by 0x or 0X. We can also use a through f instead of A to F.
Ex: 0X2, 0x9F, 0Xbcd, 0x0, 0x1. (Valid representations) Ex: Invalid representations: 0af, 0xb3g, 0Xgh.
0af: does not begin with 0x or 0X.
0xb3g, 0Xgh: illegal characters like g, h. (only a to f are allowed)

The magnitude (maximum value) of an integer constant can range from zero to some maximum value that varies from one computer to another.
Typical maximum values for most personal computers are: (16-bit machines) Decimal integer constant: 32767 (215-1) Octal integer constant: 077777 Hexadecimal integer constant: 0X7FFF
Note: The largest value that can be stored is machine dependent.

Floating point constants or Real constants : The numbers with fractional parts are called real constants.
These are the numbers with base-10 which contains either a decimal part or exponent (or both). Representation: These numbers can be represented in either decimal notation or exponent notation (scientific notation).
Decimal notation: 1234.56, 75.098, 0.0002, -0.00674 (valid notations)
Exponent or scientific notation:
General form: Mantissa e exponent
Mantissa: It is a real number expressed in decimal notation or an integer notation.
Exponent: It is an integer number with an optional plus (+)

or minus (-) sign.
E or e: The letter separating the mantissa and decimal part.
Ex: (Valid notations)

3

1.23456E+3 (1.23456×10)

1

7.5098 e+1 (7.5098×10)

-4

2E-4 (2×10)

These exponential notations are useful for representing numbers that are either very large or very small. Ex: 0.00000000987 is equivalent to 9.87e-9

Character constants:-

Single character constants: It is character(or any symbol or digit) enclosed within single quotes. Ex: „a" „1" „*"
Every Character constants have integer values known as ASCII values

ASCII:- ASCII stands for American Standard Code for Information Interchange. Pronounced ask-ee, ASCII is a code for representing English characters as numbers, with each letter assigned a number from 0 to 255.Computers can only understand numbers, so an ASCII code is the numerical representation of a character such as ‘a’ or ‘@’ or an
action of some sort.A SCII codes represent text in computers, communications equipment, and other devices that use text. Most modern character-encoding schemes are based on ASCII, though they support many additional characters. Below is the ASCII character table and this includes descriptions of the first 32 non-printing characters.

String constants or string literal:

String constant is a sequence of zero or more characters enclosed by double quotes. Example:

“MRCET” “12345” “*)(&%”

Escape Sequences or Backslash Character Constants

C language supports some nonprintable characters, as well as backslash (\ ) which can be expressed as escape sequences. An escape sequence always starts with backslash followed by one or more special characters.

For example, a new line character is represented "\n" or endl

These are used in formatting output screen, i.e. escape sequence are used in output functions.

OPERATORS AND EXPRESSIONS

An operator is a symbol which represents a particular operation that can be performed on data. An operand is the object on which an operation is performed.

By combining the operators and operands we form an expression. An expression is a sequence of operands and operators that reduces to a single value.

C operators can be classified as

1. Arithmetic operators
2. Relational operators
3. Logical operators
4. Assignment operators
5. Increment or Decrement operators
6. Conditional operator
7. Bit wise operators
8. unary operator
9. Special operators 10.Additional operators in c++

1. ARITHMETIC OPERATORS : All basic arithmetic operators are present in C. operator meaning

+ add

- subtract
* multiplication / division
% modulo division(remainder)

An arithmetic operation involving only real operands(or integer operands) is called real arithmetic(or integer arithmetic). If a combination of arithmetic and real is called mixed mode arithmetic.

```
/*C program on Integer Arithmetic Expressions*/
#include<iostraem.h> void main()
{
int a, b;
cout<"Enter any two integers"; cin>>a>>b;
cout<<"a+b"<< a+b; cout<<"a-b"<< a-b; cout<<"a*b"<< a*b;
cout<<"a/b"<< a/b; cout<<"a%b"<< a%b;
}
```

OUTPUT:

a+b=23 a-b=17 a*b=60 a/b=6 a% b=2

2. RELATIONAL OPERATORS : We often compare two quantities and depending on their relation take certain decisions for that comparison we use relational operators.

operator meaning

< is less than

> is greater than

<= is less than or equal to

>= is greater than or equal to

== is equal to

!= is not equal to

```
/* C program on relational operators*/
#include<iostream.h> void main()
{
int a,b; clrscr();
cout<<"Enter a, b values:"; cin>>a>>b; cout<<"a>b"<< a>b;
```

```
cout<<"a>=b"<< a>=b; cout<<"a<b"<< a<b; cout<<"a<=b"<<
a<=b; cout<<"a==b"<< a==b; cout<<"a!=b"<< a!=b;
} OUTPUT:
Enter a, b values: 5 9
a>b: 0 //false
a<b: 1 //true
a>=a: 1 //true
a<=b: 1 //true
a==b: 0 //false
a!=b: 1 //true
```

3. LOGICAL OPERATORS:

Logical Data: A piece of data is called logical if it conveys the idea of true or false. In C++ we use int data type to represent logical data. If the data value is zero, it is considered as false. If it is non -zero (1 or any integer other than 0) it is considered as true. C++ has three logical operators for combining logical values and creating new logical values:

```
#include<iostream.h> #include<stdbool.h> int main()
{
bool a,b;
/*logical and*/
a=0;b=0;
cout<<" a&&b "<< a&&b<<endl;
a=0;b=1;
cout<<" a&&b "<< a&&b<<endl;
a=1;b=0;
cout<<" a&&b "<< a&&b<<endl;
a=1;b=1;
cout<<" a&&b "<< a&&b<<endl;
/*logical or*/
```

```
a=0;b=0;
cout<<" a||b "<< a||b<<endl;
a=0;b=1;
cout<<" a||b "<< a||b<<endl;
a=1;b=0;
cout<<" a||b "<< a||b<<endl;
a=1;b=1;
cout<<" a||b "<< a||b<<endl;
/*logical not*/
a=0;
cout<<" a||b "<< a||b<<endl;
a=1;
cout<<" a||b "<< a||b<<endl;
return 0;
} OUTPUT:
0&&0=0
0&&1=0
1&&0=0
1&&1=1
0||0=0
0||1=1 1||0=1
1||1=1
!0 =1
!1 =0
```

4. ASSIGNMENT OPERATOR:

The assignment expression evaluates the operand on the right side of the operator (=) and places its value in the variable on the left.

Note: The left operand in an assignment expression must be a single variable. There are two forms of assignment:

- Simple assignment
- Compound assignment

Simple assignment :

In algebraic expressions we found these expressions. Ex: a=5; a=a+1; a=b+1;

Here, the left side operand must be a variable but not a constant. The left side variable must be able to receive a value of the expression. If the left operand cannot receive a value and we assign one to it, we get a compile error.

Compound Assignment:

A compound assignment is a shorthand notation for a simple assignment. It requires that the left operand be repeated as a part of the right expression. Syntax: variable operator+=value

Ex:

A+=1; it is equivalent to A=A+1;

Advantages of using shorthand assignment operator:

1. What appears on the left-hand side need not be repeated and therefore it becomes easier to write.
2. The statement is more concise and easier to read.
3. The statement is more efficient.

5.INCREMENT (++) AND DECREMENT (--) OPERATORS:

The operator ++ adds one to its operand where as the operator - - subtracts one from its operand. These operators are unary operators and take the following form: Both the increment and decrement operators may either precede or follow the operand.

Postfix Increment/Decrement :(a++/a--)

In postfix increment (Decrement) the value is incremented (decremented) by one. Thus the a++ has the same effect as a=a+1; a--has the same effect as a=a-1.

The difference between a++ and a+1 is, if ++ is after the operand, the increment takes place after the expression is evaluated.

The operand in a postfix expression must be a variable.

Ex1:
int a=5;
B=a++; Here the value of B is 5. the value of a is 6. Ex2:
int x=4; y=x--; Here the value of y is 4, x value is 3 Prefix Increment/Decrement (++a/ --a)
In prefix increment (decrement) the effect takes place before the expression that contains the operator is evaluated. It is the reverse of the postfix operation. ++a has the same effect as a=a+1.
--a has the same effect as a=a-1. Ex: int b=4;
A= ++b;
In this case the value of b would be 5 and A would be 5.
The effects of both postfix and prefix increment is the same: the variable is incremented by
1. But they behave differently when they used in expressions as shown above. The execution of these operators is fast when compared to the equivalent assignment statement.

```
#include<iostream.h> int main()
{
int a=1; int b=5;
++a;
cout<<"a="<<a<<endl;
--b;
cout<<"b="<<b<<endl;                cout<<"a="<<a++<<endl;
cout<<"a="<<a<<endl;                cout<<"b="<<b--<<endl;
cout<<"b="<<b<<endl; return 0;
}
```

a=2 b=4 a=2 a=3 b=4 b=3

6. CONDITIONAL OPERATOR OR TERNARY OPERATOR:

A ternary operator requires two operands to operate

Syntax:

```
#include<iostream.h> void main()
{
int a, b,c;
cout<<"Enter a and b values:"; cin>>a>>b;
c=a>b?a:b;
cout<<"largest of a and b is "<<c;
}
```

Enter a and b values:1 5 largest of a and b is 5

7. BIT WISE OPERATORS : C supports special operators known as bit wise operators for manipulation of data at bit level. They are not applied to float or double.

operator meaning
& Bitwise AND
^ Bitwise exclusive OR
<< left shift
>> right shift
~ one's complement

Bitwise AND operator (&)

The bitwise AND operator is a binary operator it requires two integral operands (character or integer)

Shift Operators

The shift operators move bits to the right or the left. These are of two types:

- Bitwise shift right operator
- Bitwise shift left operator

Bitwise shift right operator

It is a binary operator it requires two integral operands. The first operand is the value to be shifted and the second operand specifies the number of bits to be shifted. When bits are shifted to right,the bits at the right most end are deleted and a zero is inserted at the MSB bit.

```
#include<iostream.h>
void main()
{
int x,shift;
cout<<"Enter a number:"); cin>>x;
cout<<"enter now many times to right shift: "; cin>>shift;
cout<<"Before Right Shift:"<<x;
x=x>>shift;
cout<<"After right shift:"<<x;
}
Run1:
Enter a number:8
enter now many times to right shift:1 Before Right Shift:8
After right shift:4
```

8. SPECIAL OPERATORS

These operators which do not fit in any of the above classification are ,(comma), sizeof, Pointer operators(& and *) and member selection operators (. and ->). The comma operator is used to link related expressions together.

Operators in c++: All above operators of c language are also valid in c++.New operators introduced in c++ are:-

1. Scope Resolution operator:

Scope:-Visibility or availability of a variable in a program is called as scope. There are two types of scope.

i)Local scope ii)Global scope

Local scope: visibility of a variable is local to the function in which it is declared.

Global scope: visibility of a variable to all functions of a program Scope resolution operator in "::" .

This is used to access global variables if same variables are declared as local and global PROGRAM1.2:-

```
#include<iostream.h> int a=5;
```

```
void main()
{
int a=10;
cout<<"Local a="<<a<<endl; cout<<"Global a="<<::a<<endl;
}
```

Expected output:

Local a=10 Global a=5

Pointer to a member declarator ::*

This operator is used for declaring a pointer to the member of the class #include<iostream.h>

```
class sample
{public:
int x;
};
int main()
{ sample s; //object
int sample ::*p;//pointer decleration s.*p=10; //correct
cout<<s.*p;
}
```

Output:10

2. Pointer to member operator ->*

```
#include<iostream.h> class sample
{
public:
int x;
void display()
{
cout<<"x="<<x<<endl;
}
};
int main()
{
sample s;
```

```
sample *ptr;
//object
int sample::*f=&sample::x; s.x=10;
ptr=&s; cout<<ptr->*f; ptr->display();
}
```

3. Pointer to member operator .*

```
#include<iostream.h> class sample
{
public:
};
int x;
int main()
{
sample s; //object
int sample ::*p;//pointer decleration s.*p=10; //correct
cout<<s.*p;
}
```

Manipulators:

Manipulators are the operators used to format the data that is to be displayed on screen.The most commonly
used manipulators are endl and setw
endl:-it is used in output statement and inserts a line feed. It is similar to new line character ("\n") ex:

```
...................
cout<<"a=2"<<endl; cout<"name=sunil"<<endl;
..................
```

Output: a=2 name=sunil setw:-
this manipulator allows a specified width for a field that is to be printed on screen
and by default the value printed is right justified.This function is available in header file iomanip.h

```
#include<iostream.h> #include<iomanip.h> using namespace std; int main()
```

```
{
int s=123; cout<<"s="<<setw(10)<<s ;
}
```

output

s= 123

Insertion (<<) and Extraction (>>) operators:

the operators are use with output and input objects ex:

cout<<"Enter n"; cin>>n

Control statements:-The flow of execution of statements in a program is called as control. Control statement is a statement which controls flow of execution of the program. Control statements are classified into following categories.

1.Sequential control statements 2.Conditional control statements

3.Unconditional control statements

1. Sequential control statements:-

(type) expression;

Or

type (expression);

Sequential control

statements ensures that the instructions(or

statements) are executed in the same order in which

they appear in the program. i.e. By default system

executes the statements in the program in sequential order.

2. Conditional control statements

:Statements that are executed when a condition is true. These statements are divided into three categories. they are

1. Decision making statements 2.Switch case control statement or

3.Loop control statements or repetations

1. Decision making statements:- These statements are used to control the flow of execution of a program by making a decision depending on a condition, hence they are named

as decision making statements.

Decision making statements are of four types 1.Simple if 2. if else 3.nested if else 4.If else ladder

1. Simple if statement: if the test expression is true then if statement executes statements that immediately follow if

Syntax:

```
If(test expression)
{
List of statements;
}
```

```
/*largest of two numbers*/
#include<iostream.h> int main()
{
int a,b;
cout<<"Enter any two integers:"; cin>>a>>b;
if(a>b)
if(b>a)
cout<<"A is larger than B\n A="<<a;
cout<<"B is larger than A\n A="<<b;
return 0;
}
```

2. if –else statement:

If test expression is true block of statements following if are executed and if test expression is false then statements in else block are executed

```
if (test expression)
{
}
else
{
}
statement block1;
statement block2;
```

```
/*largest of two numbers*/
#include<iostream.h>
int main()
{
int a,b;
cout<<"Enter any two integers:"; cin>>a>>b;
if(a>b) cout<<"A is larger than B\n A="<<a; else cout<<"B is larger than A\n A="<<b;
return 0;
}
```

3. Nesting of if-else statements It's also possible to nest one if statement inside another. When a series of decisions are to be made.

If –else statement placed inside another if else statement Syntax:

```
If(test expression)
{If(test expression) {
//statements
}
else
{ //statements
}
}
else
{If(test expression) {
//statements
}
else
{ //statements
}
}
```

```
/*largest of three numbers*/ #include<iostream.h>
#include<conio.h>
```

```
int main()
{
int a,b,c;
cout<<"Enter a,b,c values:"; cin>>a>>b>>c;
if(a>b)
{
}
else
{if(b>c)
if(a>c)
{
}
else
{
}
{
cout<<"A ia largest among three numbers\n"; cout"A= "<<a;
cout<<"C ia largest among three numbers\n"; cout<<"c=
"<<c;
cout<<"B ia largest among three numbers\n";
cout<<"B="<<b;
}
getch();
}
else
{
}
cout<<"C ia largest among three numbers\n";
cout<<"c="<<c;
return 0;
}
```

4. if else ladder

```
if(condition1)
```

```
statement1; else if(condition2)
statement 2; else if(condition3)
statement n;
else
default statement.
statement-x;
```

The nesting of if-else depends upon the conditions with which we have to deal.

The condition is evaluated from top to bottom.if a condition is true the statement associated with it is executed.

When all the conditions become false then final else part containing default statements will be executed.

```
#include<iostream.h> void main()
{
int per; cout<<"Enter
percentage"; cin>>per; if(per>=80)
cout<<"Secured
Distinction"<<endl; else if(per>=60) cout<<"Secured First
Division"<<endl; else if(per>=50)
cout<<"Secured Second Division"<<endl; else if(per>=40)
cout<<"Secured Third Division"<<endl;
else cout<<"Fail"<<endl
}
```

THE SWITCH STATEMENT or MULTIWAY SELECTION :

In addition to two-way selection, most programming languages provide another selection concept known as multiway

selection. Multiway selection chooses among several alternatives. C has two different ways to implement multiway selection: the switch statement and else-if construct

If for suppose we have more than one valid choices to

choose from then we can use switch statement in place of if statements.

```
switch(expression)
{.
case value-1: case value-2:
block-1 break;
block-2 break;
default:
}
default block;
/*program to simulate a simple calculator */
#include<iostream.h> int main()
{
float a,b; char opr;
cout<<"Enter number1 operator number2 : ";
cin>>a>>oper>>b;
switch(opr)
{
case '+':
cout<<"Sum : "<<(a + b)<<endl; break;
case '-': cout<<"Difference : "<<(a -b)<<endl; break;
case '*': cout<<"Product : "<<a * b<<endl; break;
case '/': cout<<"Quotient :"<<(a / b)<<endl; break;
default: cout<<"Invalid Operation!"<<endl;
}
return 0;
}
```

Loop control statements or repetitions:

A block or group of statements executed repeatedly until some condition is satisfied is called Loop.

The group of statements enclosed within curly brace is called block or compound statement. We have two types of looping structures.

One in which condition is tested before entering the statement block called entry control. The other in which condition is checked at exit called exit controlled loop.

Loop statements can be divided into three categories as given below 1.while loop statement

2.do while loop statement 3.for loop statement

1. WHILE STATEMENT :

```
While(test condition)
{
body of the loop
}
```

It is an entry controlled loop. The condition is evaluated and if it is true then body of loop is executed. After execution of body the condition is once again evaluated and if is true body is executed once again. This goes on until test condition becomes false.

```
c program to find sum of n natural numbers */
#include<iostream.h>
int main()
{
int i = 1,sum = 0,n;
cout<<"Enter N"<<end; cin>>n;
while(i<=n)
{
sum = sum + i; i = i + 1;
}
cout<<"Sum of first"<<n<"natural numbers is:"<<sum<<endl; return 0;
}
```

2. DO WHILE STATEMENT :

The while loop does not allow body to be executed if test condition is false. The do while is an exit controlled loop and its body is executed at least once.

```
do
{
body
}while(test condition);
/*c program to find sum of n natural numbers */
#include<iostream.h>
int main()
{
int i = 1,sum = 0,n;
cout<<"Enter N"<<endl; cin>>n
do{
sum = sum + i; i = i + 1;
} while(i<=n);
cout<<"Sum of first"<< n<<" natural numbers is:"<<sum;
return 0;
}
```

Note: if test condition is false. before the loop is being executed then While loop executes zero number of times where as do--while executes one time

3. FOR LOOP : It is also an entry control loop that provides a more concise structure

Syntax:

```
for(initialization; test expression; increment/decrement)
{
statements;
}
```

For statement is divided into three expressions each is separated by semi colon;

1. initilization expression is used to initialize variables 2.test expression is responsible of continuing the loop. If it is true, then the program control flow goes inside the loop and executes the block of statements associated with it .If test expression is false loop terminates 3.increment/

decrement expression consists of increment or decrement operator This process continues until test condition satisfies.

```
/*c program to find sum of n natural numbers */
#include<iostream.h>
int main()
{
int i ,sum = 0,n;
cout<<"Enter N"; cin>>n;
for(i=1;i<=n;i++)
{
sum = sum + i;
}
cout<<"Sum of first"<<n<<" natural numbers is:%d"<<sum;
return 0;
}
```

Nested loops:Writing one loop control statement within another loop control statement is called nested loop statement

Ex:

```
for(i=1;i<=10;i++) for(j=1;j<=10;j++) cout<<i<<j;
/*program to print prime numbers upto a given number*/
#include<iostream.h>
#include<conio.h> void main()
{
int n,i,fact,j; clrscr();
cout<<"enter the number:"; cin>>n
for(i=1;i<=n;i++)
{fact=0;
//THIS LOOP WILL CHECK A NO TO BE PRIME NO. OR
NOT. for(j=1;j<=i;j++)
{
if(i%j==0) fact++;
```

```
}
if(fact==2)
cout<<i<<"\t";
}
getch( );
}
```

Output:

Enter the number : 5

2 3 5

Unconditional control statements:

Statements that transfers control from on part of the program to another part unconditionally Different unconditional statements are

1) goto 2)break 3)continue

1. goto :- goto statement is used for unconditional branching or transfer of the program execution to the labeled statement.

```
/*c program to find sum of n natural numbers */
    #include<iostream.h>
int main()
{
int i ,sum = 0,n;
cout<<"Enter N"; cin>>n;
i=1; L1:
sum = sum + i;
i++;
if(i<=n) goto L1;
cout<<"Sum of first "<<n<" natural numbers is"<<sum;
return 0;
}
```

break:-when a break statement is encountered within a loop ,loop is immediately exited and the program continues with the statements immediately following loop

```
/*c program to find sum of n natural numbers */
#include<iostream.h>
int main()
{
int i ,sum = 0,n;
cout<<"Enter N"; cin>>n;
i=1; L1:
sum = sum + i; i++;
if(i>n) break; goto L1;
cout<<"Sum of first"<<n<<"natural numbers is: "<<sum;
return 0;
}
```

Continue:It is used to continue the iteration of the loop statement by skipping the statements after continue statement. It causes the control to go directly to the test condition and then to continue the loop.

```
/*c program to find sum of n positive numbers read from
keyboard*/ #include<iostream.h>
int main()
{
int i ,sum = 0,n,number; cout<<Enter N"; cin>>n;
for(i=1;i<=n;i++)
{
cout<<"Enter a number:"; cin>>number; if(number<0)
continue; sum = sum + number;
}
cout<<"Sum of"<<n<<" numbers is:"<<sum; return 0;
}
```

CHAPTER TWO

Functions, Classes and Objects

Introduction of Class:

An object oriented programming approach is a collection of objects and each object consists of corresponding data structures and procedures. The program is reusable and more maintainable.

The important aspect in oop is a class which has similar syntax that of structure.

class: It is a collection of data and member functions that manipulate data. The data components of class are called data members and functions that manipulate the data are called member functions.

It can also called as blue print or prototype that defines the variables and functions common to all objects of certain kind. It is also known as user defined data type or ADT(abstract data type) A class is declared by the keyword class.

Syntax:-

Access Control:

Access specifier or access modifiers are the labels that specify type of access given to members of a class. These are used for data hiding. These are also called as visibility

modes. There are three types of
access specifiers
1. private 2.public 3.protected

1. Private:

If the data members are declared as private access then they cannot be accessed from other functions outside the class. It can only be accessed by the functions declared within the class. It is declared by the key word „private" .

2. public:

If the data members are declared public access then they can be accessed from other functions out side the class. It is declared by the key word „public" .

3. protected: The access level of protected declaration lies between public and private. This access specifier is used at the time of inheritance

Note:-

```
class class_name
{
Access specifier :
Variable declarations;
Access specifier :
function declarations;
};
```

Access Control:

Access specifier or access modifiers are the labels that specify type of access given to members of a class. These are used for data hiding. These are also called as visibility modes. There are three types of
access specifiers
1. private 2.public 3.protected

1. Private:

If the data members are declared as private access then they cannot be accessed from other functions outside the class. It can only be accessed by the functions declared within the class. It is declared by the key word „private" .

2. public:

If the data members are declared public access then they can be accessed from other functions out side the class. It is declared by the key word „public" .

3. protected: The access level of protected declaration lies between public and private. This access specifier is used at the time of inheritance

Note:-

```
class class_name
{
Access specifier :
Variable declarations;
Access specifier :
function declarations;
};
```

If no access specifier is specified then it is treated by default as private

The default access specifier of structure is public where as that of a class is "private"

Example:

```
class student
{
private : int roll;
char name[30];
public:
void get_data()
{
cout<<"Enter roll number and name": cin>>roll>>name;
}
```

```
void put_data()
{
cout<<"Roll number:"<<roll<<endl; cout<<"Name :"<<name<<endl;
}
};
```

Object:-Instance of a class is called object.

Syntax:

class_name object_name;

Ex:

student s;

Accessing members:-dot operator is used to access members of class

Object-name.function-name(actual arguments);

Ex:

Note:

s.get_data();

s.put_data();

1. If the access specifier is not specified in the class the default access specifier is private
2. All member functions are to be declared as public if not they are not accessible outside the class.

Object:

Instance of a class is called as object.

Syntax:

Class_name object name;

Example:

student s;

in the above example s is the object. It is a real time entity that can be used

Write a program to read data of a student

```
#include<iostream> using namespace std; class student
{
```

```
private:
int roll;
char name[20];
public:
void getdata()
{cout<<"Enter Roll number:"; cin>>roll; cout<<"Enter
Name:"; cin>>name;
}
void putdata()
{cout<<"Roll no:"<<roll<<endl;
cout<<Name:"<<name<<endl;
}
};
int main()
{
student s;
s.getdata();
s.putdata(); returm 0;
}
```

Scope Resolution operator:

Scope:-Visibility or availability of a variable in a program is called as scope. There are two types of scope. i)Local scope ii)Global scope

Local scope: visibility of a variable is local to the function in which it is declared.

Global scope: visibility of a variable to all functions of a program Scope resolution operator in "::" .

This is used to access global variables if same variables are declared as local and global

```
#include<iostream.h> int a=5;
void main()
{
int a=1;
```

```
cout<<"Local a="<<a<<endl; cout<<"Global a="<<::a<<endl;
}
```

Class Scope:

Scope resolution operator(::) is used to define a function outside a class.

```
#include <iostream> using namespace std; class sample
{
public:
void output(); //function declaration
};
// function definition outside the class void
sample::output() {
cout << "Function defined outside the class.\n";
};
int main() { sample obj; obj.output(); return 0;
}
```

Output of program:

Function defined outside the class.

Write a program to find area of rectangle

```
#include<iostream.h>
class rectangle
{
int L,B; public:
void get_data(); void area();
};
void rectangle::get_data()
{
cout<<"Enter Length of rectangle"; cin>>L;
cout<<"Enter breadth of rectangle"; cin>>B;
}
int rectangle::area()
{
return L*B;
```

```
}
int main()
{
rectangle r;
r.get_data();
cout<<"Area of rectangle is"<<r.area(); return 0;
}
```

INLINE FUNCTIONS:

Definition:

An inline function is a function that is expanded in line when it is invoked. Inline expansion makes a program run faster because the overhead of a function call and return is eliminated. It is defined by using key word "inline"

Necessity of Inline Function:

? One of the objectives of using functions in a program is to save some memory space, which becomes appreciable when a function is likely to be called many times.?

? Every time a function is called, it takes a lot of extra time in executing a series of instructions for tasks such as jumping to the function, saving registers, pushing arguments into the stack, and returning to the calling? function.

??

When a function is small, a substantial percentage of execution time may be spent in such overheads. One solution to this problem is to use macro definitions, known as macros. Preprocessor macros are popular in C. The major drawback with macros is that they are not really functions and

therefore, the usual error checking does not occur during compilation.

??

C++ has different solution to this problem. To eliminate the

cost of calls to small functions, C++
proposes a new feature called inline function.
General Form:

```
inline function-header
{
function body;
}
```

Eg:

```
#include<iostream.h>
inline float mul(float x, float y)
{
return (x*y);
}
inline double div(double p, double q)
{
return (p/q);
}
int main()
{
float a=12.345; float b=9.82;
cout<<mul(a,b); cout<<div(a,b); return 0;
}
```

Properties of inline function:

1.Inline function sends request but not a command to compiler 2.Compiler my serve or ignore the request

3.if function has too many lines of code or if it has complicated logic then it is executed as normal function

Situations where inline does not work:

? A function that is returning value , if it contains switch ,loop or both then it is treated as?
normal function.

? if a function is not returning any value and it contains a return statement then it is treated as normal function?

? If function contains static variables then it is executed as normal function?

??

If the inline function is declared as recursive function then it is executed as normal function.

Memory Allocation for Objects: Memory for objects is allocated when they are declared but not when class is defined. All objects in a given class uses same member functions. The member functions are created and placed in memory only once when they are defined in class definition

STATIC CLASS MEMBERS

Static Data Members Static Member Functions

Static Data Members:

A data member of a class can be qualified as static. A static member variable has certain special characteristics:

??

It is initialized to zero when the first object of its class is created. No other initialization is permitted.

? Only one copy of that member is created for the entire class and is shared by all the objects of that class, no matter how?

? many objects are created.?

It is visible only within the class, but its lifetime is the entire program.

? Static data member is defined by keyword „static"?

Syntax:

Data type class name::static_variable Name; Ex: int item::count;

```
#include<iostream.h> #include<conio.h> class item
{
public:
static int count; int number;
```

```
void getdata(int a)
{
number=a; count++;
}
void getcount()
{
cout<<"count is"<<count;
}
};
int item::count;//decleration int main()
{
item a,b,c;
a.getcount();
b.getcount();
c.getcount();          a.getdata(100);          b.getdata(200);
c.getdata(300); cout<<"After reading data"; a.getcount();
b.getcount();
c.getcount(); return 0;
}
```

Output: count is 0
count is 0
count is 0
After reading data count is 3
count is 3
count is 3

Static Member Functions

Like static member variable, we can also have static member functions. A member function that is declared static has the following properties:

A static function can have access to only other static members (functions or variables) declared in the same class.

A static member function is to be called using the class

name (instead of its objects) as follows: class-name :: function-name;

```
#include<iostream.h> class test
{
public:
int code;
static int count;
void setcode()
{
code=++count;
}
void showcode()
{
cout<<"object number"<<code;
}
static void showcount()
{
cout<<"count"<<count;
}
};
int test::count; int main()
{
test t1,t2;
t1.setcode();
t2.setcode(); test::showcount();
test t3;
}
t3.setcode();          test::showcount();          t1.showcode();
t2.showcode(); t3.showcode(); return 0;
```

Output:
count 2
count 3
object number 1

object number 2
object number 3

Arrays of Objects: Arrays of variables of type "class" is known as "Array of objects". An array of objects is stored inside the memory in the same way as in an ordinary array.

Syntax:

```
class class_name
{
private:
data_type members;
public:
data_type members; member functions;
};
```

Array of objects:

Class_name object_name[size]; Where size is the size of array Ex:

Myclass obj[10];

Write a program to initialize array of objects and print them #include<iostream>

```
using namespace std; class MyClass
{
int a; public:
void set(int x)
{
a=x;
}
int get()
{
return a;
}
};
int main()
{
```

```
MyClass obj[5]; for(int i=0;i<5;i++) obj[i].set(i);
for(int i=0;i<5;i++)
cout<<"obj["<<i<<"].get():"<<obj[i].get()<<endl;
}
```

Output:

```
obj[0].get():0
obj[1].get():1
obj[2].get():2
obj[3].get():3
obj[4].get():4
```

Objects as Function Arguments: Objects can be used as arguments to functions This can be done in three ways

a. Pass-by-value or call by value

b. Pass-by-address or call by address

c. Pass-by-reference or call by reference

a.Pass-by-value – A copy of object (actual object) is sent to function and assigned to the object of called function (formal object). Both actual and formal copies of objects are stored at different memory locations. Hence, changes made in formal object are not reflected to actual object. write a program to swap values of two objects

write a program to swap values of two objects

```
#include<iostream.h> using namespace std; class sample2;
class sample1
{
int a; public:
void getdata(int x);
friend void display(sample1 x,sample2 y); friend void swap(sample1 x,sample2 y);
};
void sample1::getdata(int x)
{
a=x;
```

```
}
class sample2
{
int b; public:
void getdata(int x);
friend void display(sample1 x,sample2 y);
friend void swap(sample1 x,sample2 y);
};
void sample2::getdata(int x)
{
b=x;
}
void display(sample1 x,sample2 y)
{
cout<<"Data in object 1 is"<<endl; cout<<"a="<<x.a<<endl;
cout<<"Data in object 2 is"<<endl; cout<<"b="<<y.b<<endl;
}
void swap(sample1 x,sample2 y)
{
int t;
t=x.a; x.a=y.b; y.b=t;
}
int main()
{
sample1 obj1; sample2 obj2;
obj1.getdata(5); obj2.getdata(15);
cout<<"Before Swap of data between Two objects\n ";
display(obj1,obj2);
swap(obj1,obj2);
cout<<"after Swap of data between Two objects\n ";
display(obj1,obj2);
}
```

Before Swap of data between Two objects Data in object 1

is a=5
Data in object 2 is b=15
after Swap of data between Two objects Data in object 1 is a=5
Data in object 2 is b=15

b. Pass-by-address: Address of the object is sent as argument to function.

Here ampersand(&) is used as address operator and arrow (->) is used as de referencing operator. If any change made to formal arguments then there is a change to actual arguments write a program to swap values of two objects

```
#include<iostream.h>
using namespace std; class sample2;
class sample1
{
int a; public:
void getdata(int x);
friend void display(sample1 x,sample2 y); friend void swap(sample1 *x,sample2 *y);
};
void sample1::getdata(int x)
{
a=x;
}
class sample2
{
int b; public:
void getdata(int x);
friend void display(sample1 x,sample2 y); friend void swap(sample1 *x,sample2 *y);
};
void sample2::getdata(int x)
{
```

```
b=x;
}
void display(sample1 x,sample2 y)
{
cout<<"Data in object 1 is"<<endl; cout<<"a="<<x.a<<endl;
cout<<"Data in object 2 is"<<endl; cout<<"b="<<y.b<<endl;
}
void swap(sample1 *x,sample2 *y)
{
int t;
t=x->a;
x->a=y->b; y->b=t;
}
int main()
{
sample1 obj1; sample2 obj2;
obj1.getdata(5); obj2.getdata(15);
cout<<"Before Swap of data between Two objects\n ";
display(obj1,obj2);
swap(&obj1,&obj2);
cout<<"after Swap of data between Two objects\n ";
display(obj1,obj2);
}
```

Before Swap of data between Two objects Data in object 1 is a=5

Data in object 2 is b=15

after Swap of data between Two objects Data in object 1 is a=15

Datatype & reference variable =variable;

Data in object 2 is b=5

c.Pass-by-reference:A reference of object is sent as argument to function.

Reference to a variable provides alternate name for

previously defined variable. If any change made to reference variable then there is a change to original variable.

A reference variable can be declared as follows

Ex:

```
int x=5; int &y=x;
```

Write a program to find sum of n natural numbers using reference variable #include<iostream.h>

```
using namespace std;
int main()
{
int i=0; int &j=i; int s=0; int n;
cout<<"Enter n:"; cin>>n; while(j<=n)
{
s=s+i; i++;
}
cout<<"sum="<<s<<endl;
}
```

Output:

Enter n:10 sum=55

write a program to swap values of two objects

```
#include<iostream.h> using namespace std; class sample2;
class sample1
{
int a; public:
void getdata(int x);
friend void display(sample1 x,sample2 y); friend void swap(sample1 &x,sample2 &y);
};
void sample1::getdata(int x)
{
a=x;
}
```

```
class sample2
{
int b; public:
void getdata(int x);
friend void display(sample1 x,sample2 y); friend void
swap(sample1 &x,sample2 &y);
};
void sample2::getdata(int x)
{
b=x;
}
void display(sample1 x,sample2 y)
{
cout<<"Data in object 1 is"<<endl; cout<<"a="<<x.a<<endl;
cout<<"Data in object 2 is"<<endl; cout<<"b="<<y.b<<endl;
}
void swap(sample1 &x,sample2 &y)
{
int t;
t=x.a; x.a=y.b; y.b=t;
}
int main()
{
sample1 obj1; sample2 obj2;
obj1.getdata(5); obj2.getdata(15);
cout<<"Before Swap of data between Two objects\n ";
display(obj1,obj2);
swap(obj1,obj2);
cout<<"after Swap of data between Two objects\n ";
display(obj1,obj2);
}
```

Output:

Before Swap of data between Two objects Data in object 1

is a=5
Data in object 2 is b=15
after Swap of data between Two objects Data in object 1 is a=15
Data in object 2 is b=5

FRIEND FUNCTIONS:The private members cannot be accessed from outside the class. i.e.... a non member function cannot have an access to the private data of a class. In C++ a non member function can access private by making the function friendly to a class.

Definition:

A friend function is a function which is declared within a class and is defined outside the class. It does not require any scope resolution operator for defining . It can access private members of a class. It is declared by using keyword "friend"

Ex:

```
class sample
{
int x,y; public:
sample(int a,int b); friend int sum(sample s);
};
sample::sample(int a,int b)
{
x=a;y=b;
}
int sum(samples s)
{
int sum;
sum=s.x+s.y; return 0;
}
void main()
{
```

```
Sample obj(2,3); int res=sum(obj);
cout<< "sum="<<res<<endl;
}
```

A friend function possesses certain special characteristics:

? It is not in the scope of the class to which it has been declared as friend.?

? Since it is not in the scope of the class, it cannot be called using the object of that class. It can be invoked like a normal?
function without the help of any object.

? Unlike member functions, it cannot access the member names directly and has to use an object name and dot?
membership operator with each member name.

? It can be declared either in the public or private part of a class without affecting its meaning.?

? Usually, it has the objects as arguments.?

```
#include<iostream.h> class sample
{
int a; int b; public:
void setvalue()
{ a=25; b=40;
}
friend float mean(sample s);
};
float mean(sample s)
{
return float(s.a+s.b)/2.0;
}
int main()
{
sample X;
X.setvalue();
cout<<"Mean value="<<mean(X); return 0;
```

}

write a program to find max of two numbers using friend function for two different

classes #include<iostream> using namespace std;

```
class sample2; class sample1
{
int x; public:
sample1(int a);
friend void max(sample1 s1,sample2 s2)
};
sample1::sample1(int a)
{
x=a;
}
class sample2
{
int y; public:
sample2(int b);
friend void max(sample1 s1,sample2 s2)
};
Sample2::sample2(int b)
{
y=b;
}
void max(sample1 s1,sample2 s2)
{
If(s1.x>s2.y)
cout<<"Data member in Object of class sample1 is larger "<<endl;
else
}
cout<<"Data member in Object of class sample2 is larger "<<endl;
```

```
void main()
{
sample1 obj1(3); sample2 obj2(5); max(obj1,obj2);
}
```

Write a program to add complex numbers using friend function

```
#include<iostream>
using namespace std; class complex
{
float real,img; public:
complex(); complex(float x,float y)
friend complex add_complex(complex c1,complex c2);
};
complex::complex()
{
real=img=0;
}
complex::complex(float x,float y)
{
real=x;img=y;
}
complex add_complex(complex c1,complex c2)
{
complex t;
t.real=c1.real+c2.real; t.img=c1.img+c2.img; return t;
}
void complex::display ()
{
if(img<0)
{img=-img;
cout<<real<<"-i"<<img<<endl
}
else
{
```

```
}
}
cout<<real<<"+i"<<img<<endl
int main()
{
complex obj1(2,3); complex obj2(-4,-6);
complex obj3=add_compex(obj1,obj2); obj3.display();
return 0;
}
```

Friend Class:A class can also be declared to be the friend of some other class. When we create a friend class then all the member functions of the friend class also become the friend of the other class. This requires the condition that the friend becoming class must be first declared or defined (forward declaration).

```
#include <iostream.h> class sample_1
{
public:
friend class sample_2;//declaring friend class int a,b;
void getdata_1()
{
cout<<"Enter A & B values in class sample_1"; cin>>a>>b;
}
void display_1()
{
cout<<"A="<<a<<endl; cout<<"B="<<b<<endl;
}
};
class sample_2
{
public:
int c,d,sum; sample_1 obj1;
void getdata_2()
```

```
{
obj1.getdata_1();
cout<<"Enter C & D values in class sample_2"; cin>>c>>d;
}
void sum_2()
{
sum=obj1.a+obj1.b+c+d;
}
void display_2()
{
cout<<"A="<<obj1.a<<endl;      cout<<"B="<<obj1.b<<endl;
cout<<"C="<<c<<endl;           cout<<"D="<<d<<endl;
cout<<"SUM="<<sum<<endl;
}
};
int main()
{
sample_1 s1;
s1.getdata_1(); s1.display_1();
sample_2 s2;
s2.getdata_2(); s2.sum_2(); s2.display_2();
}
```

Enter A & B values in class sample_1:1 2 A=1
B=2
Enter A & B values in class sample_1:1 2 3 4 Enter C & D values in class sample_2:A=1 B=2
C=3 D=4 SUM=10

CHAPTER THREE

Constructors, Destructors, Inheritance

Introduction to Constructors: C++ provides a special member function called the constructor which enables an object to initialize itself when it is created.

Definition:- A constructor is a special member function whose task is to initialize the objects of its class. It is special because its name is the same name as the class name. The constructor is invoked whenever an object of its associated class is created. It is called constructor because it constructs

the values of data members of the class. A constructor is declared and defined as follows:

```
    class integer
{
int m,n; public: integer( );
...........
...........
};
integer :: integer( )
{
```

```
m=0; n=0;
}
    int main()
{ integer obj1;
...........
...........
}
```

integer obj1; => not only creates object obj1 but also initializes its data members m and n to zero. There is no need to write any statement to invoke the constructor function.

CHARACTERISTICS OF CONSTRUCTOR

? They should be declared in the public section.?

? They are invoked automatically when the objects are created.?

? They do not have return type, not even void.?

? They cannot be inherited, though a derived class can call the base class constructor.?

? Like other c++ functions, they can have default arguments.?

? Constructors cannot be virtual.?

??

We cannot refer to their addresses.

??

They make „implicit calls" to the operators new and delete when memory allocation is required.

Constructors are of 3 types:

1. Default Constructor
2. Parameterized Constructor
3. Copy Constructor

1. Default Constructor: A constructor that accepts no parameters is called the default constructor.

```
#include<iostream.h>
#include<conio.h> class item
{
int m,n; public: item()
{
m=10; n=20;
}
void put();
};
void item::put()
{
cout<<m<<n;
}
void main()
{
item t; t.put();
getch();
}
```

2. Parameterized Constructors:-The constructors that take parameters are called
parameterized constructors. #include<iostream.h>

```
class item
{
int m,n; public:
item(int x, int y)
{
m=x; n=y;
}
};
```

When a constructor has been parameterized, the object declaration statement such as
item t; may not work. We must pass the initial values as arguments to the constructor function when an object is

declared. This can be done in 2 ways: item t=item(10,20);
//explicit call
item t(10,20); //implicit call

Eg:
```
#include<iostream.h> #include<conio.h> class item
{
int m,n; public:
item(int x,int y)
{
m=x; n=y;
}
void put();
};
void item::put()
{
cout<<m<<n;
}
void main()
{
item t1(10,20);
item t2=item(20,30); t1.put();
t2.put();
getch();
}
```

3. Copy Constructor: A copy constructor is used to declare and initialize an object from another object.

Eg:
```
item t2(t1); or
item t2=t1;
```

1. The process of initializing through a copy constructor is known as copy initialization.
2. t2=t1 will not invoke copy constructor. t1 and t2 are objects, assigns the values of t1 to t2.
3. A copy constructor takes a reference to an object of the

same class as itself as an argument. #include<iostream.h>

```
class sample
{
int n; public:
sample()
{ n=0;
}
sample(int a)
{
n=a;
}
sample(sample &x)
{
n=x.n;
}
void display()
{
cout<<n;
}
};
void main()
{
sample A(100); sample B(A); sample C=A; sample D;
D=A;
A. display();
B. display();
C. display();
D. display();
}
```

Output: 100 100 100 100

Multiple Constructors in a Class: Multiple constructors can be declared in a class. There can be any number of constructors in a class.

```
class complex
{
float real,img; public:
complex()//default constructor
{
real=img=0;
}
complex(float r)//single parameter parameterized
constructor
{
real=img=r;
}
complex(float r,float i) //two parameter parameterized
constructor
{
real=r;img=i;
}
complex(complex&c)//copy constructor
{
real=c.real; img=c.img;
}
complex sum(complex c )
{
complex t; t.real=real+c.real; t.img=img+c.img; return t;
}
void show()
{
If(img>0)
cout<<real<<"+i"<<img<<endl;
else
}
};
{
```

```
img=-img;
cout<<real<<"-i"<<img<<endl;
}
void main()
{
complex c1(1,2); complex c2(2,2); compex c3;
c3=c1.sum(c3); c3.show();
}
```

DESTRUCTORS:A destructor, is used to destroy the objects that have been created by a constructor.

Like a constructor, the destructor is a member function whose name is the same as the class name but is preceded by a tilde.

Eg: ~item() { }

1. A destructor never takes any argument nor does it return any value.
2. It will be invoked implicitly by the compiler upon exit from the program to clean up storage that is no longer accessible.
3. It is a good practice to declare destructors in a program since it releases memory space for future use.

```
#include<iostream> using namespace std; class Marks
{
public:
int maths; int science;
//constructor Marks() {
cout << "Inside Constructor"<<endl;
cout << "C++ Object created"<<endl;
}
//Destructor
class derived-class-name : visibility-mode base-class-name
{
.........
```

```
.........
}
~Marks() {
cout << "Inside Destructor"<<endl;
cout << "C++ Object destructed"<<endl;
}
};
int main( )
{
Marks m1; Marks m2; return 0;
}
```

Output:

Inside Constructor C++ Object created Inside Constructor C++ Object created Inside Destructor C++ Object destructed Inside Destructor C++ Object destructed

INHERITANCE: . The mechanism of deriving a new class from an old one is called inheritance or derivation. The old class is referred to as the base class and the new one is called the derived class or sub class. The derived class inherits some or all of the traits from the base class.

A class can also inherit properties from more than one class or from more than one level.Reusability is an important feature of OOP

A derived class can be defined by specifying its relationship with the base class in addition to its own details.

Thc colon indicates that the derived class name is derived from the base-class-name. the visibility mode is optional and if present, may be either private or protected or public. The default is private. Visibility mode specifies whether the features of the base class are privately derived or publicly derived.

class ABC : private XYZ

```
{
members of ABC;
};
//private derivation
class ABC:public XYZ
{
members of ABC;
};
//public derivation
class ABC:protected XYZ {
// protected derivationmembers of ABC;
};
class ABC:XYZ //private by default
{
members of ABC;
};
```

When a base class is privately inherited by a derived class, public members of the base class can only be accessed by the member functions of the derived class.private membes of base class are inaccessible to the objects of the derived class

When a base class is protected inherited by a derived class, public members of the base class can only be accessed by the member functions of the derived class.private membes of base class are inaccessible to the objects of the derived class. If private members of base class are to be inherited to derived class then declare them as protected

When the base class is publicly inherited, public members of the base class is publicly inherited, public members of the base class become public members of the derived class and therefore they are accessible to the objects of the derived class. In both the cases, the private members are not inherited and therefore, the private members of a base

class will never become the members of its derived class
In inheritance, some of the base class data elements and member functions are „inherited" into the derived class. We can add our own data and member functions and thus extend the functionality of the base class. Inheritance, when used to modify and extend the capability of the existing classes, becomes a very powerful tool for incremental program development
Types of Inheritance: 1.Single Inheritance 2.Multi level Inheritance 3.Mutiple Inheritance 4.Hybrid inheritance
5. Hierarchical Inheritance.
1.SINGLE INHERITANCE: one derived class inherits from only one base class. It is the most simplest form of Inheritance.

```
/ /Base class
//Derived class
#include<iostream> using namespace std; class A
{
public:
int a,b; void get()
{
cout<<"Enter any two Integer values"<<endl; cin>>a>>b;
}
};
class B:public A
{
int c; public:
void add()
{
c=a+b; cout<<a<<"+"<<b<<"="<<c;
}
};
```

```
int main()
{
B b; b.get();
b.add();
}
```

Output:

Enter any two Integer values 1 2

1+2=3

A

B

A

B

C

2. MULTILEVEL INHERITANCE: In this type of inheritance the derived class inherits from a class, which in turn inherits from some other class. The Super class for one, is sub class for the other.

```
#include<iostream.h> class A
{
public:
int a,b; void get()
{
cout<<"Enter any two Integer values"<<endl; cin>>a>>b;
}
};
class B:public A
{
public:
int c;
void add()
{
c=a+b;
}
```

```
};
class C:public B
{
public:
void show()
{ cout<<a<<"+"<<b<<"="<<c;
}
};
int main()
{
C c;
c.get();
c.add();
c.show();
}
```

Output:

Enter any two Integer values 12 14

12+14=26

3. Multiple Inheritance:In this type of inheritance a single derived class may inherit from two or more than two base classes.

Syntax:

```
class D : visibility A, visibility B,....
{
..................
}
#include<iostream.h> class A
{
public: int a;
};
class B
{
public:
```

```
};
void getA()
{
cout<<"Enter an Integer value"<<endl; cin>>a;
}
int b;
void getB()
{
cout<<"Enter an Integer value"<<endl; cin>>b;
}
class C:public A,public B
{
public: int c;
void add()
{
c=a+b; cout<<a<<"+"<<b<<"="<<c<<endl;
}
};
int main()
{
C obj; obj.getA();
obj.getB();
obj.add();
}
```

Enter an Integer value 12 Enter an

A

B

C

A

B

C

D

Integer value 13

12+13=25

4. Hybrid Inheritance: Hybrid inheritance is combination of two or more inheritances such as single,multiple,multilevel or Hierarchical inheritances.

```
#include<iostream.h> class arithmetic
{
protected:
int num1, num2;
public:
};
void getdata()
{
cout<<"For Addition:"; cout<<"\nEnter the first number: ";
cin>>num1;
cout<<"\nEnter the second number: "; cin>>num2;
}
class plus:public arithmetic
{
protected:
int sum;
public:
};
void add()
{
sum=num1+num2;
}
class minus
{
protected:
int n1,n2,diff;
public:
void sub()
{
```

```
cout<<"\nFor Subtraction:"; cout<<"\nEnter the first
number: "; cin>>n1;
cout<<"\nEnter the second number: ";
A
B
C
D
cin>>n2; diff=n1-n2;
}
};
class result:public plus, public minus
{
public:
void display()
{
cout<<"\nSum of "<<num1<<" and "<<num2<<"= "<<sum;
cout<<"\nDifference of "<<n1<<" and "<<n2<<"= "<<diff;
}
};
int main()
{
result z;
z.getdata();
z.add();
z.sub();
z.display();
}
```

For Addition:

Enter the first number: 1 Enter the second number: 2

For Subtraction:

Enter the first number: 3 Enter the second number: 4

Sum of 1 and 2= 3

Difference of 3 and 4= -1

5. Hierarchical Inheritance:- Inheriting is a method of inheritance where one or more derived classes is derived from common base class.

```
#include<iostream.h> class A //Base Class
{
public:
int a,b;
void getnumber()
{
cout<<"\n\nEnter Number :\t"; cin>>a;
}
};
class B : public A //Derived Class 1
{
public:
void square()
{
getnumber(); //Call Base class property cout<<"\n\n\
tSquare of the number :\t"<<(a*a);
}
};
class C :public A //Derived Class 2
{
public:
void cube()
{
getnumber(); //Call Base class property cout<<"\n\n\
tCube of the number :::\t"<<(a*a*a);
}
};
int main()
{
B b1; //b1 is object of Derived class 1 b1.square(); //call
```

member function of class B C c1; //c1 is object of Derived class 2 c1.cube(); //call member function of class C
}
Enter Number : 2
Square of the number : 4 Enter Number : 3
Cube of the number ::: 27

CHAPTER FOUR

Pointers, Virtual Functions and Polymorphism

Introduction to Memory Management:

DYNAMIC MEMORY ALLOCATION & DEALLOCATION (new & delete)

C uses malloc() and calloc() functions to allocate memory dynamically at run time. It uses the function free() to deallocated dynamically allocated memory.

C++ supports these functions, it defines two unary operators new and delete that perform the task of allocating and deallocating the memory in a better and easier way.

A object can be created by using new, and destroyed by using delete.

A data object created inside a block with new, will remain in existence until it is explicitly
destroyed by using delete.

new operator:-

new operator can be used to create objects of any type .Hence new operator allocates sufficient memory to hold data of objects and it returns address of the allocated memory. Syntax:

Ex: int *p = new int;

Ex: int *p = new int[10];
delete operator:
If the variable or object is no longer required or needed is destroyed by "delete" operator, there by some amount of memory is released for future purpose. Synatx:
Eg: delete p;

If we want to free a dynamically allocated
array: delete [size] pointer-variable;
Program: write a program to find sum of list of integers
#include<iostream> using namespace std; int main()
{
int n,*p;
To create memory space for arrays:
pointer-variable = new data-type[size];
cout<<"Enter array size:"; cin>>n;
p=new int[n];
cout<<"Enter list of integers"<<endl; for(int i=0;i<n;i++)
cin>>p[i];
//logic for summation int s=0;
for(int i=0;i<n;i++)
s=s+p[i];
cout<<"Sum of array elements is\n"; cout<<s;
delete [ ]p; return 0;
}
Enter array size:5 Enter list of integers 1 2 3 4 5
Sum of array elements is 15
Member Dereferencing operator:-
1.
Pointer to a member declarator
::*

2.
Pointer to member operator
->*
3.
Pointer to member operator
.*
Pointer to a member declarator ::*
This operator is used for declaring a pointer to the member of the class

```
#include<iostream.h>
class sample
{public:
int x;
};
int main()
{ sample s; //object
int sample ::*p;//pointer decleration s.*p=10; //correct
cout<<s.*p;
}
```

Output:10

2. Pointer to member operator ->*

```
#include<iostream.h> class sample
{
public:
int x;
void display()
{
cout<<"x="<<x<<endl;
}
};
int main()
{
sample s; //object
sample *ptr;
```

```
int sample::*f=&sample::x;
s.x=10;
ptr=&s; cout<<ptr->*f; ptr->display();
}
```

3. Pointer to member operator .*

```
#include<iostream.h> class sample
{
public:
};
int x;
int main()
{
sample s; //object
int sample ::*p;//pointer decleration s.*p=10; //correct
cout<<s.*p;
}
```

Pointers to Obj?ects:Pointers to objects are useful for creating objects at run time. To access members arrow operator ( ) and de referencing operator or indirection (*) are used.

Declaration of pointer.

className*ptr

ex:

item *obj;

Here obj is a pointer to object of type item.

```
class item
{
public:
int code; float price;
void getdata(int a,float b)
{
code=a; price=b;
}
```

```
void show()
{
cout<<"code:"<<code<<"\n"<<"Price:"<<price<<endl;
}
};
```

Declaration of object and pointer to class item:

```
item obj;
item *ptr=&obj;
```

The member can be accessed as follow.

a) Accessing members using dot operator obj.getdata(101,77.7); obj.show();

b) using pointer

ptr->getdata(101,77.7); ptr->show();

c) Using de referencing operator and dot operator (*ptr).getdata(101,77.7);

(*ptr).show();

Creating array of objects using pointer: item *ptr=new item[10];

Above declaration creates memory space for an array of 10 objects of type item.

```
#include<iostream.h> class item
{
public:
int code; float price;
void getdata(int a,float b)
{
code=a; price=b;
}
void show()
{
cout<<code<<"\t"<<price<<endl;
}
};
```

```
int main()
{
int n; int cd;
float pri;
cout<<"Enter number of objects to be created:"; cin>>n;
item *ptr=new item[n]; item *p;
p=ptr;
for(int i=0;i<n;i++)
{
cout<<"Enter data for object"<<i+1; cout<<"\nEnter
Code:";cin>>cd; cout<<"Enter price:";cin>>pri;
p->getdata(cd,pri); p++;
}
p=ptr;
cout<<"Data in various objects are "<<endl; cout<<"Sno\
tCode\tPrice\n"; for(i=0;i<n;i++)
{
}
return 0;
}
cout<<i+1<<"\t"; ptr->show(); ptr++;
```

Pointers to Derived Classes: Pointers can be declared to derived class. it can be used to access members of base class and derived class. A base class pointer can also be used to point to object of derived class but it can access only members that are inherited from base class.

```
#include<iostream.h> class base
{
public:
int a;
void get_a(int x)
{
a=x;
```

```
}
void display_a()
{
cout<<"In base"<<"\n"<<"a="<<a<<endl;
}
};
class derived:public base
{
int b; public:
void get_ab(int x,int y)
{
a=x; b=y;
}
void display_ab()
{
cout<<"In Derived "<<"\n"<<"a="<<a<<"\nb="<<b<<endl;
}
};
int main()
{
base b; base *bptr;
bptr=&b;//points to the object of base class bptr-
>get_a(100);
bptr->display_a();
derived d; derived *dptr;
dptr=&d;//points to the object of derived class
dptr->get_a(400);
Polymorphism
Run time
Compile time
Polymorphism
Polymorphism
dptr->display_a();
```

```
dptr->get_ab(300,200); dptr->display_ab();
bptr=&d;//points to the object of derived class bptr-
>get_a(400);
bptr->display_a();
return 0;
}
```

Output:

In base a=100

In base a=400

In Derived

a=300 b=200

In base

a=400

RUNTIME POLYMORPHISM USING VIRTUAL FUNCTIONS

Static & Dynamic Binding

Polymorphism means „one name" -„multiple forms.

The overloaded member functions are „selected" for invoking by matching arguments, both type and number. This information is known to the compiler at the compile time and compiler is able to select the appropriate function for a particular call at the compile time itself. This is called Early Binding or Static Binding or Static Linking. Also known as compile time polymorphism. Early binding means that an object is bound to its function call at the compile time.

It would be nice if the appropriate member function could be selected while the program is running. This is known as runtime polymorphism. C++ supports a mechanism known as virtual function to achieve run time polymorphism.

At the runtime, when it is known what class objects are under consideration, the appropriate version of the function is invoked. Since the function is linked with a particular class much later after the compilation, this process is termed as late binding. It is also known as dynamic binding because the selection of the appropriate function is done dynamically at run time.

Virtual Functions

Operator Overloading

Function Overloading

VIRTUAL FUNCTIONS

Polymorphism refers to the property by which objects belonging to different classes are able to respond to the same message, but different forms. An essential requirement of polymorphism is therefore the ability to refer to objects without any regard to their classes.

When we use the same function name in both the base and derived classes, the function in the bas class is declared as virtual using the keyword virtual preceding its normal declaration.

When a function is made virtual, C++ determines which function to use at runtime based on the type of object pointed to by the base pointer, rather than the type of the pointer. Thus, by making the base pointer to point to different objects, we can execute different versions of the virtual function.

```
#include<iostream.h> class Base
{
public:
void display()
{
cout<<"Display Base";
}
virtual void show()
{
```

```
cout<<"Show Base";
}
};
class Derived : public Base
{
public:
void display()
{
cout<<"Display Derived";
}
void show()
{
cout<<"show derived";
}
};
void main()
{
Base b;
Derived d;
Base *ptr;
cout<<"ptr points to Base"; ptr=&b;
ptr->display(); //calls Base ptr->show(); //calls Base
cout<<"ptr points to derived"; ptr=&d;
ptr->display(); //calls Base ptr->show(); //class Derived
}
```

Output:

ptr points to Base

Display Base Show Base

ptr points to Derived Display Base

Show Derived

When ptr is made to point to the object d, the statement ptr->display(); calls only the function associated with the Base i.e.. Base::display()

where as the statement ptr->show();
calls the derived version of show(). This is because the function display() has not been made virtual in the Base class.

Rules For Virtual Functions:

When virtual functions are created for implementing late binding, observe some basic rules that satisfy the compiler requirements.

1. The virtual functions must be members of some class.
2. They cannot be static members.
3. They are accessed by using object pointers.
4. A virtual function can be a friend of another class.
5. A virtual function in a base class must be defined, even though it may not be used.
6. The prototypes of the base class version of a virtual function and all the derived class versions must be identical. C++ considers them as overloaded functions, and the virtual function mechanism is ignored.
7. We cannot have virtual constructors, but we can have virtual destructors.
8. While a base pointer points to any type of the derived object, the reverse is not true. i.e. we cannot use a pointer to a derived class to access an object of the base class type.
9. When a base pointer points to a derived class, incrementing or decrementing it will not make it to point to the next object of the derived class. It is incremented or decrementcd only relative to its base type. Therefore we should not use this method to move the pointer to the next object.
10. If a virtual function is defined in the base class, it need not be necessarily redefined in the derived class. In such cases, calls will invoke the base function.

OVERLOADING

OPERATOR OVERLOADING

C++ has the ability to provide the operators with as special meaning for a data type. The mechanism of giving such special meanings to an operator is known as operator overloading. We can overload all the operators except the following:

Class member access operator ("." And "
.*") Scope resolution operator "::"
Size operator (sizeof) Conditional operator

To define an additional task to an operator, specify what it means in relation to the class to which the operator is applied. This is done with the help of a special function, called operator function.

The process of overloading involves following steps:

1. Create a class that defines the data type that is to be used in the overloading operation.
2. Declare the operator function operator op() in the public part of the class. It may be a member function or a friend function.
3. Here op is the operator to be overloaded.
4. Define the operator function to implement the required operations.

Ex:

```
complex complex::operator+(complex c)
{
complex t;
t.real=real+c.real; t.img=img+c.img; return t;
}
```

Concept of Operator Overloading

One of the unique features of C++ is Operator Overloading. Applying overloading to operators means, same operator in responding different manner. For example operator + can be used as concatenate operator as well as additional operator.

That is 2+3 means 5 (addition), where as "2"+"3" means 23 (concatenation).

Performing many actions with a single operator is operator overloading. We can assign a user defined function to an operator. We can change function of an operator, but it is not recommedned to change the actual functions of operator. We can't create new operators using this operatorloading.

Operator overloading concept can be applied in following two major areas (Benefits)

1. Extension of usage of operators
2. Data conversions

Rules to be followed for operator overloading:-

1. Only existing operators can be overloaded.
2. Overloaded operators must have at least one operand that is of user defined operators 3.We cannot change basic meaning of an operator.
4. Overloaded operator must follow minimum characteristics that of original operator
5. When using binary operator overloading through member function, the left hand operand must be an object of relevant class

The number of arguments in the overloaded operator" s arguments list depends

1. Operator function must be either member function or friend function.

General Form:-

```
return-type classname :: operator op(arglist)
{
Function body
}
```

2. If operator function is a friend function then it will have one argument for unary operator & two arguments for binary operator

3. If operator function is a member function then it will have Zero argument for unary operator & one arguments for binary operator

Unary Operator Overloading

An unary operator means, an operator which works on single operand. For example, ++ is an unary operator, it takess single operand (c++). So, when overloading an unary operator, it takes no argument (because object itself is considered as argument).

Syntax for Unary Operator (Inside a class)

```
return-type operator operatorsymbol( )
{
//body of the function
}
```

Ex:

```
void operator-()
{
real=-real; img=-img;
}
```

Syntax for Unary Operator (Outside a class)

```
return-type classname::operator operatorsymbol( )
{
//body of the function
}
```

Example 1:-

```
void operator++()
{
counter++;
}
```

Example 2:-

```
void complex::operator-()
{
real=-real; img=-img;
}
```

The following simple program explains the concept of unary overloading.

```
#include < iostream.h > #include < conio.h >
// Program Operator Overloading class fact
{
int a;
public:
fact ()
{
a=0;
}
fact (int i)
{
a=i;
}
fact operator!()
{
int f=1,i; fact t;
for (i=1;i<=a;i++)
{
f=f*i;
}
t.a=f; return t;
}
void display()
{
cout<<"The factorial "<< a;
}
};
```

```
void main()
{
int x;
}
cout<<”enter a number”; cin>>x;
fact s(x),p; p=!s; p.display();
```

Output for the above program:

Enter a number 5

The factorial of a given number 120

Explanation:

We have taken „!“ as operator to overload. Here class name is fact. Constructor without parameters to take initially value of „x“ as 0. Constructor with parameter to take the value of „x“ . We have create two objects one for doing the factorial and the other for return the factorial. Here number of parameter for an overloaded function is 0. Factorial is unary operator because it operates on one dataitem. operator overloading find the factorial of the object. The display function for printing the result.

Overloading Unary Operator -

Example 1:-

Write a program to overload unary operator –

```
#include<iostream> using namespace std; class complex
{
float real,img; public:
complex();
complex(float x, float y); void display();
void operator-();
};
complex::complex()
{
real=0;img=0;
```

```
}
complex::complex(float x, float y)
{
real=x; img=y;
}
void complex::display()
{
int imag=img;
if(img<0)
{
imag=-img;
cout<<real<<" -i"<<imag<<endl;
}
else
cout<<real<<" +i"<<img<<endl;
}
void complex::operator-()
{
real=-real; img=-img;
}
int main()
{
complex c(1,-2);
c.display();
cout<<"After Unary - operation\n";
-c; c.display();
}
```

Example 2:- #include<iostream.h> using namespace std;

```
class space
{
int x,y,z; public:
void getdata(int a,int b,int c); void display();
```

It is possible to overload a unary minus operator using a

friend function as follows:

```
friend void operator-(space &s);
void operator-();
};
void space :: getdata(int a,int b,int c)
{
x=a; y=b; z=c;
}
void space :: display()
{
cout<<"x="<<x<<endl;                    cout<<"y="<<y<<endl;
cout<<"z="<<z<<endl;
}
void space :: operator-()
{
x=-x;
y=-y;
z=-z;
}
int main()
{
space s; s.getdata(10,-20,30); s.display();
-s;
cout<<"after negation\n"; s.display();
}
```

Output: x=10 y=-20 z=30
after negation x=-10
y=20 z=-30

Example 3:-

Unary minus operator using a friend function

```
#include<iostream.h>        #include<iostream.h>        using
namespace std; class space
{
```

```
int x,y,z; public:
Syntax for Binary Operator (Inside a class)
return-type operator operatorsymbol(argument)
{
//body of the function
}
void getdata(int a,int b,int c); void display();
friend void operator-(space &);
};
void space :: getdata(int a,int b,int c)
{
x=a; y=b; z=c;
}
void space :: display()
{
cout<<x<<" "<<y<<" "<<z<<endl;
}
void operator-(space &s)
{
s.x=-s.x;
s.y=-s.y;
s.z=-s.z;
}
int main()
{
space S; S.getdata(10,-20,30); S.display();
-S;
cout<<"after negation\n"; S.display();
}
```

Output:

10 -20 30

after negation

-10 20-30

Binary Operator Overloading

An binary operator means, an operator which works on two operands. For example, + is an binary operator, it takes single operand (c+d). So, when overloading an binary operator, it takes one argument (one is object itself and other one is passed argument).

Example

```
complex operator+(complex s)
{
complex t; t.real=real+s.real; t.img=img+s.img; return t;
}
```

The following program explains binary operator overloading: #include < iostream.h >

```
#include < conio.h > class sum
{
int a; public:
sum()
{
a=0;
}
sum(int i)
{
}
a=i;
sum operator+(sum p1)
{
sum t;
}
void main ()
{
t.a=a+p1.a; return t;
cout<<"Enter Two Numbers:" int a,b;
cin>>a>>b; sum x(a),y(b),z; z.display(); z=x+y;
```

```
cout<<"after applying operator \n"; z.display();
getch();
}
```

Output for the above program:

Enter two numbers 5 6 After applying operator

Syntax for Binary Operator definition (Outside a class)

```
return-type classname::operator
operatorsymbol(argument)
{
//body of the function
}
```

The sum of two numbers 11

Explanation: The class name is „sum" . We have create three objects two for to do the sum and the other for returning the sum. " +" is a binary operator operates on members of two objects and returns the result which is member of a object.here number of parameters are 1. The sum is displayed in display function.

Write a program to over load arithmetic operators on complex numbers using member function

```
#include<iostream.h> class complex
{
public:
float real,img;
complex(){ } complex(float x, float y)
{
real=x; img=y;
}
complex operator+(complex c) void display();
};
complex complex::operator+(complex c)
{
```

```
complex temp;
temp.real=real+c.real; temp.img=img+c.img; return temp;
}
void complex::display()
{
int imag=img;
If(img<0)
{
}
else
}
imag=-imag; cout<<real<<"-i"<<imag;
cout<<real<<"+i"<<img;
int main()
{
complex c1,c2,c3;
c1=complex(2.5,3.5);    c2=complex(1.6,2.7);    c3=c1+c2;
c3.display();
return 0;
}
```

Overloading Binary Operators Using Friends

1. Replace the member function declaration by the friend function declaration in the class friend complex operator+(complex, complex)
2. Redefine the operator function as follows:

```
complex operator+(complex a, complex b)
{
return complex((a.x+b.x),(a.y+b.y));
}
```

Write a program to over load arithmetic operators on complex numbers using friend function

```
#include<iostream.h>
class complex
```

```
{
public:
float real,img;
complex(){ } complex(float x, float y)
{
real=x; img=y;
}
friend complex operator+(complex); void display();
};
complex operator+(complex c1, complex c2)
{
complex temp;
temp.real=c1.real+c2.real; temp.img=c1.img+c2.img; return
temp;
}
void complex::display()
{
If(img<0)
{
}
else
}
img=-img; cout<<real<<"-i"<<img;
cout<<real<<"+i"<<img;
int main()
{
complex c1,c2,c3;
c1=complex(2.5,3.5);    c2=complex(1.6,2.7);    c3=c1+c2;
c3.display();
return 0;
}
```

CHAPTER FIVE

Templates and Exception handling

GENERIC PROGRAMMING(Templates)

Generic programming is an approach where generic types are used as parameters in algorithms so that they work for a variety of suitable data types and data structures.

A significant benefit of object oriented programming is reusability of code which eliminates redundant coding. An important feature of C++ called templates strengthens this benefit of OOP and provides great flexibility to the language. Templates support generic programming, which allows to develop reusable software components such as functions, classes etc.. supporting different data types in a single framework.

Templates Concept Introduction

Instead of writing different functions for the different data types, we can define common

function. For example

int max(int a,int b); // Returns maximum of two integers

float max(float a,float b); // Return maximum of two floats

char max(char a,char b); // Returns maximum of two characters (this is called as function overloading)

But, instead of writing three different functions as above,

C++ provided the facility called "Templates". With the help of templates you can define only one common function as follows:

T max(T a,T b); // T is called generic data type

Template functions are the way of making function/class abstracts by creating the behavior of function without knowing what data will be handled by a function. In a sense this is what is known as “generic functions or programming”.

Template function is more focused on the algorithmic thought rather than a specific means of single data type. For example you could make a templated stack push function. This push function can handle the insertion operation to a stack on any data type rather then having to create a stack push function for each different type.

Syntax:

```
template < class type >
ret_type fun_name(parameter list)
{
--------------//body of function
} //www.suhritsolutions.com
```

Features of templates:-

1. It eliminates redundant code
2. It enhances the reusability of the code.
3. It provides great flexibility to language Templates are classified into two types. They are

1. Function templates 2.Class Templates. Function Templates

The templates declared for functions are called as function templates. A function template defines how an individual function can be constructed.

Syntax :

```
template < class type,.........> ret _type fun_
```

```
name(arguments)
{
-----------------// body of the function
}
```

CLASS TEMPLATES

The templates declared for classes are called class templates. A class template specifies how individual classes can be constructed similar to the normal class specification. These classes model a generic class which support similar operations for different data types. General Form of a Class Template

```
template <class T> class class-name
{
.......
.......
};
```

A class created from a class template is called a template class. The syntax for defining an object of a template class is:

```
classname<type> objectname(arglist);
#include<iostream.h> #include<conio.h> template <class
T> class swap
{
T a,b;
public: swap(T x,T y)
{
a=x; b=y;
}
void swapab()
{
T temp;
temp=a; a=b; b=temp;
}
```

```
void showdata()
{
cout<<a<<b;
}
};
void main()
{
int m,n; float m1,n1;
cout<<"Enter integer values"; cin>>m>>n;
cout<<"Enter floating values"; cin>>m1>>n1;
swap<int> c1(m,n); swap<float> c2(m1,n1); c1.swapab();
c1.showdata(); c2.swapab(); c2.showdata();
}
```

Class Template with Multiple Parameters

Syntax:

```
template <class T1, class T2,....> class class-name
{
.......
.......
}
```

```
#include<iostream.h> template <class T1,class T2> class
Test
{
T1 a; T2 b;
public:
Test(T1 x,T2 y)
{
a=x; b=y;
}
void show()
{
cout<<a<<b;
}
```

```
};
void main()
{
Test<float,int>        test1(1.23,123);        Test<int,char>
test2(100,"w"); test1.show();
test2.show();
}
```

FUNCTION TEMPLATES

Like class template we can also define function templates that would be used to create a family of functions with different argument types.

General Form:

```
template <class T>
return-type function-name (arguments of type T)
{
.........
.........
}
```

```
#include<iostream.h> template<class T>
void swap(T &x, T &y)
{
T temp = x; x=y; y=temp;
}
void fun(int m,int n,float a,float b)
{
cout<<m<<n;   swap(m,n);   cout<<m<<n;   cout<<a<<b;
swap(a,b); cout<<a<<b;
}
int main()
{ fun(100,200,11.22,33.44);
return 0;
}
```

Example 2:-

```
#include < iostream.h > #include < conio.h > template
T max(T a, T b)
{
if(a>b)
return a; else
return b;
}
void main( )
{
}
output:
char ch1,ch2,ch3;
cout<<"enter two characters"<< ch2<< ch3;
cin>>ch2>>ch3;
d=max(ch2,ch3); cout<<"max(ch2,ch3)"<< ch1; int a,b,c;
cout<<"enter two integers:"; cin>>a>>b;
c=max(a,b); cout<<"max(a,b):"<< c<< endl; float f1,f2,f3;
cout<<"enter two floats< f1f2 >:"; cin>>f1,f2;
f3=max(f1,f2); cout<<"max(f1,f2):"<< f3;
```

enter two characters: A,B max(ch2,ch3):B

enter two integers:20,10 max (a,b) :20

enter two floats :20.5,30.9 max (f1,f2) :30.9

Function Template with Multiple Parameters

Like template class, we can use more than one generic data type in the template statement, using a comma-separated list as shown below:

```
template <class T1, class T2,.> return-type function-name(arguments of types T1,T2.) {
........
........
}
#include<iostream.h> #inlcude<string.h> template<clas T1,
```

```
class T2> void display(T1 x,T2 y)
{
cout<<x<<y;
}
int main()
{
display(1999,"EBG"); display(12.34,1234); return 0;
}
```

Exception handling

Exceptions: Exceptions are runtime anomalies or unusual conditions that a program may encounter while executing .Anomalies might include conditions such ass division by zero, accessing an array outside of its bounds or running out of memory or disk space. When a program encounters an exception condition, it must be identified and handled.

Exceptions provide a way to transfer control from one part of a program to another. C++ exception handling is built upon three keywords: try, catch, and throw.

Types of exceptions:There are two kinds of exceptions

1.Synchronous exceptions

2. Asynchronous exceptions

1. Synchronous exceptions:Errors such as "Out-of-range index" and "over flow" are synchronous exceptions

2. Asynchronous exceptions: The errors that are generated by any event beyond the control of the program are called asynchronous exceptions

The purpose of exception handling is to provide a means to detect and report an exceptional circumstance

Exception Handling Mechanism:

An exception is said to be thrown at the place where some error or abnormal condition is detected. The throwing will cause the normal program flow to be aborted, in a raised exception. An exception is thrown programmatic, the programmer specifies the conditions of a throw.

In handled exceptions, execution of the program will resume at a designated block of code, called a catch block, which encloses the point of throwing in terms of program execution. The catch block can be, and usually is, located in a different function than the point of throwing.

C++ exception handling is built upon three keywords: try, catch, and throw.

Try is used to preface a block of statements which may generate exceptions. This block of statements is known as try block. When an exception is detected it is thrown by using throw statement in the try block. Catch block catches the exception thrown by throw statement in the try block and handles it appropriately.

```
#include<iostream> using namespace std; int main()
{
int a,b;
cout<<"Enter any two integer values"; cin>>a>>b;
int x=a-b;
try
{
if(x!=0)
{
cout<<"Result(a/x)="<<a/x<<endl;
}
else
{
throw x;
}
}
catch(int ex)
{
cout<<"Exception caught:Divide By Zero \n";
```

}
}

THROWING MECHANISM

When an exception is detected, it can be thown by using throw statement in any one of the following forms

? throw(exception);?

? throw exception;?

??

throw;

CATCHING MECHANISM:

Catch block is as below Catch(data type arg)

```
{
//statements for handling
//exceptions
}
```

Multiple catch statements:

```
try
{
//try block
}
catch(data type1 arg)
{
//catch block1
}
catch(data type2 arg)
{
//catch block2
}
..................
................. catch(data typeN arg)
{
//catch blockN
}
```

• When an exception is thrown, the exception handler are searched in order fore an appropriate match.

• It is possible that arguments of several catch statements match the type of an exception. In such cases the first handler that matches the exception type is executed

Write a Program to catch multiple catch statements

```
#include<iostream.h>
void test(int x)
{
try
{
}
if(x==1) throw x; else
if(x==0) throw 'x'; else
if(x==-1) throw 1.0;
cout<<"end of try block"<<endl;
catch(char c)
{
cout<<"caught a character"<<endl;
}
catch(int m)
{
cout<<"caught an integer"<<endl;
}
catch(double d)
{
cout<<"caught a double"<<endl;
}
}
int main()
{
test(1);
test(0);
```

```
test(-1);
test(2); return 0;
}
```

Output:

caught an integer caught a character caught a double end of try block

Catch All Exceptions:

all possible types of exceptions and therefore may not be able to design independent catch handlers to catch them. In such circumstances, we can force a catch statement to catch all exceptions instead of a certain type alone.

```
catch(...)
{
.........
}
```

Write a Program to catch all exceptions

```
#include<iostream.h>
void test(int x)
{
try
{
if(x==0) throw x; if(x==0) throw 'x'; if(x==-1) throw 1.0;
}
catch(...)
{
cout<<"caught exception"<<endl;
}
}
int main()
{
test(-1);
test(0);
test(1);
```

```
return 0;
}
```

Re-throwing an Exception:

It is possible to pass exception caught by a catch block again to another exception handler. This I known as Re-throwing.

```
#include <iostream> using namespace std; void
MyHandler()
{
try
{
throw "hello";
}
catch (const char*)
{
cout <<"Caught exception inside MyHandler\n"; throw;
//rethrow char* out of function
}
}
int main()
{
cout<< "Main start ... "<<endl;
try
{
MyHandler();
}
catch(const char*)
{
cout <<"Caught exception inside Main\n";
}
cout << "Main end"; return 0;
}
```

Specifying Exceptions:

Specification of exception restrict functions to throw some

specified exceptions only with the use of throw(exception list) in the the header of the function.

General form

```
Type function_name(argument list) throw(exceptions
-list)
{
Statements try
{
statements
}
}
```

```
#include <iostream> using namespace std;
void test(int x) throw(int,float,char)
{
switch(x)
{
case 1:throw x;
break; case 2:throw 'x';
break; case 3:throw double(x);
break; case 4:throw float(x);
break;
}
}
int main()
{
try
{
test(4);//test(4) leads to abnormal termination
}
catch(int i)
{
cout <<"Caught int type exception\n";
}
```

```
catch(float f)
{
cout <<"Caught float type exception\n";
}
catch(char c)
{
cout <<"Caught char type exception\n";
}
catch(double i)
{
cout <<"Caught Double type exception\n";
}
return 0;
}
```

A programming language is a vocabulary and set of grammatical rules for instructing a computer or computing device to perform specific tasks.

The term programming language usually refers to high-level languages, such as BASIC, C, C++, COBOL, Java, FORTRAN, Ada, and Pascal.

9 798886 298673

Printed by Libri Plureos GmbH in Hamburg,
Germany